Report Of The Proceedings Of The North Walsham Farmers' Club, From Its Commencement To ... 1843...

North Walsham farmers' club

REPORT OF THE PROCEEDINGS

OF THE

NORTH WALSHAM

FARMERS' CLUB,

FROM ITS

COMMENCEMENT TO THE PRESENT TIME.

1843.

Norwich:

BACON, KINNEBROOK, AND CO. MERCURY OFFICE.

MDCCCXLIII.

REPORT.

In conformity with a motion carried unanimously, and entered on the minutes of the Society, "That a Report of the proceedings of the North Walsham Farmers' Club, during the last three years, be drawn up and printed for distribution amongst the members," the Committee beg to state, they have examined the minutes recorded by the Secretary, together with sundry other documents, and have framed their Report upon the principle of classing the several subjects which came before the Club under their respective heads, rather than by taking them in the order they may have been discussed at sundry periods; but before they enter upon this duty, your Committee beg to express the deep sense they entertain of the obligation the Society is under to the Hon. W. R. Rous, not only for his valuable services as Chairman of the "North Walsham Farmers' Club," but also for his ready support and zealous co-operation in the furtherance of such measures as may have for their object the advancement of agriculture as a science—the profitable employment of capital in the cultivation of the soil—the ameliorating the moral and social condition of labourers in husbandry, and of creating employment for the rural population at large. They have also to congratulate the Society on the progress it has already made in disseminating practical and useful information amongst its members, and more especially on the introduction of a measure which has for its object, not only to promote the interest of the corn grower and the grazier, but to open a wide field for the investment of capital, and an unbounded scope for the employment of a redundant population.

It will readily be perceived that your Committee allude to the cultivation of linseed, a new production to be engrafted upon the system of our native husbandry.

This measure was taken up and introduced to the North Walsham Farmers' Club by one of its members, as an experiment, the object of which was to ascertain whether, and to what extent it might be practicable, to substitute native produce for a portion at least of the oil cake, hitherto used as cattle food and manure, procured from foreign countries. The experiment was attended with as much success as could reasonably be expected from a measure which can only be determined by practical demonstrations; a question which can only be decided by experiments still to be made, bearing upon very important considerations relative to the outlay of capital; the advantage of substituting one kind of grain for another, and to what extent this may affect the present system of cropping; the fattening quality of the food employed for the purpose of grazing, and the comparative value of the manure procured from both the one and the other.

In drawing up this Report, your Committee beg to state that they regard the introduction of linseed into our system of native husbandry (together with its concomitants, the preparation and manufacture of Flax) as a measure of so much importance, that it will eventually redound to the credit of the Eastern Division of this County, and to the members of the " North Walsham Farmers' Club," as being the first to set it on foot, and they have been careful to record the circumstances attending its progress down to that period which ended in the establishment of " The Norfolk Flax Society."

The subject was first brought under consideration in December, 1841, when the attention of the Society was directed to advantages which might be expected to accrue from crushing and boiling grain and pulse for the purpose of feeding cattle, with a view to lessen the consumption of foreign oil cake; at which meeting it was unanimously agreed that experiments should be instituted to ascertain the practicability of this measure, which appeared worthy of the consideration and adoption of the Society. In conformity with this resolution, sundry experiments were tried by several members, amongst which the following deserve more particularly to be noticed.

Six pigs, the same size, breed, and character were put to the test of being fattened on baked mange wurzel, mixed up with a small quantity of boiled barley, the result of which experiment appeared to be highly satisfactory, but as it was not then brought to a conclusion, your Committee has no certain data to offer under that head.

The trial of the comparative merits of feeding cart horses on corn, baked swede turnips, and baked mangel wurzel, afforded a most convincing proof of the superiority of the latter, since, although those horses which were fed on the two former did their work without any perceptible alteration in their condition, yet those which were put upon the latter had so much improved at the end of a fortnight, that the difference between the one and the other was clearly perceptible.

During the time the horses were subjected to these experiments in diet, they were employed, with but little intermission, in carting clay; and the weekly allowance of those which were fed on corn, was a bushel of oats or barley to each horse; and those which were fed on cooked roots had about 10 bushels of turnips or mangel wurzel each, together with an unlimited quantity of hay and chaff.

The next experiment referred to, was the result of a trial in feeding two hogs on boiled barley and two on barley meal.

The pigs were weighed and placed in separate sties, and at the expiration of three weeks were weighed again.

The advantage proved to be considerably in favour of barley meal. The pigs fed on meal consumed 2 coombs, 2 bushels, and 2½ pecks of barley, and increased in weight 6 stones and 4 lbs. Those fed on boiled barley consumed 1 coomb, 2 bushels, and half a peck, and increased in weight 3 stones and 2 lbs.

The respective weights were :—

HOGS FED ON BOILED BARLEY.

	1st weight.	2nd weight.	Increase.
No. 1. ..	126 lbs. ..	148 lbs.	} 3 st. 2 lbs.
No. 2. ..	108 lbs. ..	130 lbs.	

HOGS FED ON BARLEY MEAL.

No. 3. ..	112 lbs. ..	156 lbs.	} 6 st. 4 lbs.
No. 4. ..	116 lbs. ..	160 lbs.	

It ought to be observed that the failure in the experiment relative to the boiled barley, may be attributed to the fact, that a large portion of the grain passed through the pigs without having been sufficiently masticated or properly digested. To this cause and to the quantity of water taken up by the whole barley over and above that which is absorbed by barley meal, may in some measure account for the marked superiority of the one over the other. Hogs are gross feeders, and in this particular are perhaps ill-adapted to profitable feeding with any other than such food as requires but little or no mastication, and is the most readily digested. This failure appeared to the member who tried the experiment an exception to the general rule, since it was stated by him that he had proved to his own satisfaction, that every other description of live stock would thrive and fatten upon boiled barley. It appears, however, to be ill-adapted for the fattening of fowls, arising in all probability from the gluten with which the grain is intermixed by the process of boiling, rendering the mass too compact and adhesive for the fowls to swallow.

The discussion on the best method of feeding sheep having in some measure failed to produce that interest which the subject required, in consequence of the absence of the member who proposed to introduce it, the Meeting simply came to the conclusion that the system of cutting turnips, and consuming them in troughs, was the most economical, the most expeditious, and the most efficacious method of grazing sheep.

The cultivation of green crops was a subject brought before the meeting, in which it was shewn that one acre of grass mowed and consumed in the yard or stall, was equal to three acres fed off where it had grown. It was also deemed highly important to have a succession of crops, for summer feeding; such for instance as rye to begin with, then vetches, and lastly vetches dibbled in a layer of either clover or nonsuch, by which method an immense increase in the bulk and quality of the green food was obtained. It was therefore resolved that stall-feeding was by far the most economical and profitable method of feeding cattle, especially if the importance of the superior quality and extra quantity of the manure obtained thereby is taken into consideration.

During the progress of these experiments, and the discussions which the subject called forth, it appears to your Committee that the proposition of adding a portion of linseed to the corn or pulse, was casually suggested and immediately adopted. It is stated in a pamphlet, published in April, 1842, that " the desirableness of fattening cattle on home-made food, rather than on foreign produce, was a subject brought forward at one of those (the North Walsham Farmers' Club) meetings, in consequence of which a series of experiments were made, by incorporating linseed with corn or pulse, in sundry proportions, which ended in the production of the desired substitute for foreign oil cake."

At this time the subject had been taken up by sundry individuals, and considered so important, that a special meeting was convened for the 19th of May in that year, " for the purpose of enquiring into the results of experiments made by several members of the Club, in grazing bullocks with linseed compounds," to which the public were invited to attend. This meeting took place in the Bear

Inn yard, at North Walsham, where coppers had been erected for the purpose of making compound; at which time specimens of linseed, the produce of our own soil, were also exhibited.

Cattle fattened on compound, by several members of the Club, were shown, as well as some others fattened on oil cake, which, having been inspected by the public, the meeting adjourned to the great room, where the Hon. W. R. Rous opened the business by stating the object for which they were met, pointing out the importance of the enquiry, as involving the question whether we could fatten cattle from the produce of our own soil, or whether we were to continue dependant upon foreigners. Several members who had exhibited stock or had tried the experiment of feeding with compound *versus* oil cake, delivered their sentiments on the occasion in favour of the former, and replied to the questions put to them by other individuals not connected with the Society; the result of which was, that a very favourable impression was imparted to the public on this momentous question.

At this period of the proceedings, a challenge was given by the "North Walsham Farmers' Club" to the county at large, to test the merit of their compound in the following manner, namely:—That a given number of beasts, carefully selected by competent judges, should be put to keeping at the same time, by parties opposed to each other; one lot to be fed on compound and turnips, and the other on oil cake, which beasts should eventually be exhibited to the public.

This challenge was not accepted, in consequence of which Mr. Postle, of Smallburgh, undertook to determine the question himself, by an experiment made with twelve bullocks, the result of which your Committee will have to relate hereafter.

In framing this Report, your Committee beg leave to observe, that their object is to record the proceedings of the North Walsham Farmers' Club as a whole, rather than to particularize the contributions of any individual member thereof. They feel, however, that in two or three instances, it will be necessary to depart from this principle. The name of WARNES is inseparably connected with the subject now under consideration, and in tracing out the brief history of the introduction of LINSEED, and the purposes to which it may be applied, their object is to shew to what extent the Society claims for itself the honour of bringing it into notice, in conjunction with Mr. Warnes, and in doing this, your Committee beg to express the deep sense they entertain of the valuable co-operation of that gentleman, and the industrious perseverance with which he has, in his own behalf, as well as that of the Society, endeavoured to promote this desirable object, to which end they cannot do better than transcribe the speech of Mr. Warnes, as delivered at the meeting in question, and repeated in the columns of "the Norwich Mercury."

Mr. Warnes, jun. said, "allow me to express my thanks to you, Sir, and to the North Walsham Farmers' Club, for the promptness with which you acceded to my wishes in convening this special meeting; for after the exhibitions which we have this afternoon witnessed, the most prejudiced, captious, and incredulous mind must, I think, acquit me of having made exaggerated statements in those letters which appeared in the public papers. The subject has met with very gratifying attention from various parts of the kingdom. I have therefore been anxious to afford the best information on the subject, by private as well as by public correspondence, and I have reason to believe, if the resolution which I hold in my hand be carried by this meeting, the system which it advocates will speedily be adopted by a vast majority of the agriculturists of this kingdom.

"By the rules of this Society, strangers are permitted to take part in our discussions, but not to vote. On this particular occasion strangers are not only invited to state their candid opinions of our proceedings, but to record those opinions with the votes of the members themselves. It is in fact a public meeting, called together for a public purpose, since our object is to arrive at right conclusions.

"The question of fattening, &c. is one of national importance; it affects a multitude of interests, and merits the strongest corroborating testimony that can be obtained. Had the question been merely of an individual character, affecting only particular interests, there would have been no necessity for the present meeting. Those who have made use of the cattle compound are convinced of the advantages derived from it over the use of oil cake. But these advantages are, and ever must remain, confined to very narrow limits, until the main body of British farmers shall be induced to substitute home grown and home made food to fatten cattle, instead of food made and grown on a foreign soil. Then may we calculate upon obtaining a higher price for our barley, and a more profitable return for our beasts. These are the considerations which hang on the importance of feeding cattle on native oil cake, and I think a brief review of the last fatal season for the sale of barley, and of meal, will in some measure prove the correctness of my calculations.

"The reason assigned for the low price of barley was an immense excess of supply over demand. A precisely opposite reason was assigned for the high price of oil cakes, for the demand exceeded the supply. The farmer at one time had, I believe, to accept from 10*l.* to 12*l.* per last for his barley, and to pay down 10*l.* to 12*l.* per ton for oil cake. Now, gentlemen, had our mode of converting barley into cattle food been in full operation, the turnip crop could have been economized, and thousands of coombs of barley saved, and, for aught I know, double the price obtained for that which was sold at market. I verily believe, that every coomb of barley consumed by cattle would have been a clear saving, and returned to the pocket in the sale of the meat. I contend that all the surplus barley has this year been worse than thrown away, since the money that it sold for was given to the foreigner—to the encouragement of foreign agriculture, and to the employment of foreign labourers. Not one guinea of all those sums of money paid by the farmers of this county to the farmers of a foreign country, for oil cake, has found its way back to the pockets of the former—the whole has been sunk—it is lost and gone for ever. So long as the farmers of this country encourage the introduction of foreign oil cake, the effect in future years will be the same as the past. The great drawback on the profits of grazing is the cost of oil cake. The great drawback on the profits of farming is a bad price for barley. If there ever was a period when it was necessary to alter our system, that period has arrived. For the ports are opened at a less rate of duty, and, consequently, the surplus barley will be infinitely greater, and the price, of course, infinitely lower.

"To whatever quarter we turn, there we find the demand for barley lessened every year. The maltster tells us that he cannot dispose of his malt. The merchant assures us that he can find no sale for barley. While others exclaim—Oh, the habits of the people are so changed, that barley will be less in request than ever. Evidently the produce of barley exceeds the demand; therefore we must turn our attention to the cultivation of something else.

"To the score of foreign cake must be added, the quantity of linseed imported and manufactured into cake, swelling the amount, perhaps to double the quantity, and consequently has a tendency to double the quantity of overplus barley.

"It will be seen, that 10,000 of coombs of foreign barley were indirectly imported in the shape of oil cake and of linseed, and consumed by British farmers, instead of barley of their own growth.

Now, that which applies to barley is equally applicable to meat; for all the meat that is raised by feeding cattle on foreign oil cake, must, of necessity, be the produce of a foreign country. Therefore, amongst the various reasons assigned for the low price of beasts, and for the unprofitable return of our own fat bullocks, I am persuaded that the main cause centres in the unlimited use of foreign oil cake, rather than of native produce.

"I am inclined to believe, that this important question will not be allowed to rest with the North Walsham Farmers' Club, but that it will be discussed throughout the British nation; and I even flatter myself so far as to calculate upon the time when we shall find our club united with the intelligent, the affluent, the influential, and the industrious agriculturists, in one common determination to fatten cattle on native produce, and not lend a helping hand to the mischievous effects of the corn bill and the tariff, by being ourselves the importers of beef and barley, in the shape of foreign oil cake. The benefits to be derived from this question appears to me as inexhaustible as the advantages are incalculable. The employment of our labourers ranks amongst the most prominent of those advantages. Under the present system of using food of foreign make to fatten cattle, we necessarily contribute largely to the maintenance of foreign labourers, but by making it at home, we shall find ample employment for our own.

"What legislators have failed in discovering we have an opportunity of accomplishing, viz.—the finding of employment for the redundant rural population of the whole kingdom, *through the simple means of the cultivation of linseed, and forming the seed into food to fatten cattle.*

"Mr. Warnes then moved a resolution to the effect, that the price of barley was materially lowered by the consumption of foreign oil cake, and that the Society, as well as the strangers present, would use home produce instead of foreign."

This admirable introduction of the subject matter, delivered by Mr. Warnes, met with universal approbation, except that an objection was taken relative to the fairness of attributing the low price of barley wholly to the use of oil cake, since the experience of former years would put a negative to that assumption. And with regard to the expectation entertained by Mr. Warnes, that the compound would supersede the use of oil cake, it was stated by a member who had frequently visited those districts on the Continent where linseed is extensively cultivated, that he had counted as many as 200 crushing mills driven by wind, from the ramparts at Lisle only, which circumstance, he observed, would convey some idea of the extent to which linseed is cultivated in Flanders and the Netherlands ; and if we consider that the importation of foreign cake in the year 1840 amounted to 73,104 tons, and in 1841 to 75,564 tons, we might easily conceive that the cultivation of that article was a subject of too much importance on the other side of the Channel to be readily abandoned. Moreover should we succeed in perfecting the preparation of British compound so as to bring it into general use, the circumstance would only create a change in the system pursued abroad, and would have no effect in preventing its introduction in any other shape. Some years since oil cake was used in Holland as an article of fuel, but would they revert to that alternative now ? On the contrary, the new tariff afforded additional facilities for exporting oil cake, a component part of their staple commodity— linseed in the shape of corn and beef ; consequently if we refuse to accept the raw material for the purpose of converting it into one or other of these articles, they will send them to us in their manufactured state ; nevertheless, he continued, there is one very important feature in the cultivation of linseed to which no allusion has been made in the speech delivered by Mr. Warnes ; namely, *the value of the fibre!!* Singularly enough, that gentleman afterwards admitted that at this time he did not even know that flax was obtained from the stem of the plant in question. Thus a new idea was furnished to that gentleman, of which he availed himself to its fullest extent, as we shall have occasion to observe hereafter.

Your Committee do not now deem it expedient to afford a detailed account of the condition of the cattle exhibited at this meeting, which had been fed on compound, because, as the respectable Editor of the Norwich Mercury at that time observed, " an experiment is nothing if it be not exact, and although in this case it is perhaps unnecessary to insist upon extreme nicety, still there appeared to us a want of that exactitude as to the material points which in such a case it is so necessary for the farmer to know, before he can determine as to the superiority of the one food over the other."

These points have since been investigated through the medium of an experiment, conducted with that degree of exactitude which will set the question of Compound *versus* Oil Cake completely at rest, as we shall hereafter have occasion to explain.

Your Committee have now brought their Report of the proceedings of " The North Walsham Farmers' Club," relative to the growth of linseed, down to the period that an especial meeting was convened " for the purpose of enquiring into the results of experiments made by several members of the club, in grazing bullocks with linseed compounds instead of oil cake ;" but they have also to remark that other cattle in a less forward condition were exhibited with a view (as it was then intimated) to produce the same cattle at the Society's next annual meeting, in order that the public might be better able to judge of the merits of the compound by the improved condition of the beasts during the interval ; to which end, and with a view to forming a society for promoting the cultivation of linseed, the following notice appeared in the Norwich Mercury and the Norfolk Chronicle.

NORTH WALSHAM FARMERS' CLUB.
The Hon. W. R. Rous, President.

The public are most cordially invited to the annual meeting and dinner of this Society, on Friday, the 28th instant. To guard against unfavourable weather, Spanton's booth will be erected, and ample shelter afforded on the grounds of the Rev. W. F. Wilkinson, near the town. The bullocks shewn at the special meeting on the 19th of May last, will, with an eleven-month-old calf, be again exhibited and afterwards slaughtered, in order to afford the most accurate information respecting the fattening properties of native produce when formed into compound. Specimens of the food upon which they have been fed, with the process of making it, will be submitted to the closest inspection, and every particular respecting the cost and quantity consumed fully communicated. Steam apparatus upon a new and simple construction for cooking farm produce will be seen at work ; also a variety of machines for crushing linseed and grain.

Between twenty and thirty samples of linseed, flax in straw, and specimens of wrought flax of Norfolk growth, will be arranged in the booth ; and at two o'clock the company will assemble to inquire into the desirableness of forming a society to extend and improve the cultivation of that important plant.

The Committee of Management hope that gentlemen and farmers in the neighbourhood will kindly send for exhibition specimens of turnips, mangel-wurzel, carrots, potatoes, &c. &c. and any description of live stock that may tend to advance the interest of agriculture. Notice to be given to Mr. Cubitt, Librarian to the Club, North Walsham, a few days previous to the meeting, in order that proper arrangements may be made for their reception and classification.

Dilham, Oct. 5, 1842.　　　　　　　　G. GOWER, Hon. Sec.

The interest excited by this announcement and invitation, drew together a very large and respectable assemblage of persons, including the Members of the Eastern Division of the County, and many other Gentlemen and Landed Proprietors, as well as Occupiers.

The Rev. W. F. Wilkinson had very kindly allowed the Society to make use of a paddock and farming premises belonging to him in the vicinity of the town.

Spanton's booth was erected on this spot, and sundry steaming and cooking apparatus, built in masonry, erected at the expence of the Club, were employed in preparing the compound, according to the following methods, recommended by Mr. Warnes, and explained both verbally and practically by the men employed in preparing the compound for the information of the public, of which the following detailed account is taken from a pamphlet published and distributed on the same day :—

" Let a quantity of linseed be reduced to fine meal, and barley to the thickness of a wafer, by a bruising or a crushing machine with smooth cylinders. Put 168 pounds of water into an iron cauldron, commonly called a copper, and as soon as it boils, not before, stir in twenty-one pounds of linseed meal; continue stirring it for about five minutes; then let sixty-three pounds of the crushed barley be sprinkled by the hand of one person upon the boiling musilage, while another rapidly stirs and crams it in; after the whole has been carefully incorporated, which will not occupy more than five minutes, cover it closely down and throw the furnace door open. Should there be too much fire, put it out. The mass will continue to simmer, from the heat of the cauldron, till the barley has entirely absorbed the musilage. The work is then complete, and the food may be used on the following day. When removed into tubs, it must be rammed down, to exclude the air, and to prevent its turning rancid. After a little practice, the eye will be a sufficient guide to the proportions, without the trouble of weighing.

" The process is very simple, and is fit employment for women, or infirm men. It will be seen that these proportions consist of three parts of barley to one of linseed, and of two parts of water to one of barley and linseed included. Also, that the weight of the whole is 18 stone when put into the cauldron, but after it has been made into compound, and become cold, the weight will be found in general reduced to something less than 15 stone, which afford one bullock, for a fortnight, a stone per day, containing one pound and a half of linseed. It will keep a long time, if properly prepared. The consistency ought to be like that of clay when made into bricks.

" In the spring and summer months, germinated barley might be made into compound with great advantage. Bullocks will eat it with avidity, and thrive very fast upon it. The process is very simple. Let some barley be steeped about two days, and the water drained off; after the radical or root has grown to nearly a quarter of an inch in length, it must be well bruised with the crushing machine, and as much as possible forced into some boiling musilage, containing the same quantity of linseed, but a fourth less of water than would have been prepared for dry barley. It will soon turn sour, but the cattle will not refuse it on that account. Care must be taken lest the sprouts are suffered to grow beyond the prescribed length, or the quality will be materially injured ; therefore it will be necessary to check their growth, either by spreading the barley about the floor or by running it through the crusher; it may then be used at pleasure. A different treatment must be observed in making compound with peas. Barley, as I have shewn, will readily absorb the oily matter from the linseed by simple immersion when boiling ; but peas require to be boiled first, and the linseed added afterwards. To every pailful of peas put into the cauldron, about three pails of water is to be added. The peas must be boiled till they yield, when nipped, a mealy substance, not unlike baked or boiled potatoes. The water by this time will have nearly disappeared. A convenient portion of peas should then be put into a stout-bottomed trough, with a small quantity of the liquor and a little linseed, which are to be immediately mashed with a rammer by a man, while a boy turns them over. This quantity being soon sufficiently united, remove it into a tub. The remaining portions are to be prepared in the same way. As the mass increases in the tub, it should be pressed firmly down with the rammer, in order that it may retain the heat as long as possible. Should there be more liquor in the copper than is required for mashing, it may be put by degrees into the tub with the mashed peas and linseed. The length and size of the rammer ought to be adapted to the height and strength of the person employed. It will be found convenient to have two or three at hand, varying from eighteen inches to two feet long, tapering, and from four to six inches square at the bottom. A pin should be passed through the top for the convenience of working it with both hands at once. Peas will take less time to boil after they have been steeped a few hours; but observe they will not require so much water in the cauldron as if dry. Another plan of making compound with peas is to steep them eight or ten hours, then drain off the water, and when dry externally pass them through the crusher, the rollers set closer the second time, so as to reduce them to something like a mealy consistency. Sometimes they can be sufficiently bruised by the first operation. Put equal quantities of this meal and water, by measure, into the cauldron; let them boil about twenty minutes; then add a fourth or fifth of linseed meal to the quantity of peas, treating it precisely in the same way required for barley compound. The extreme ease with which peas are crushed after being steeped will fully compensate for the trouble. Smooth rollers will scarcely make any impression on hard peas, and the labour is excessive. Light and ordinary wheat may profitably be consumed according to this system; but as it is very adhesive when cooked, a mixture of barley will be found beneficial. It is to be crushed in the same way as barley, but will carry more water."

Your Committee have the more minutely described these several processes recommended by Mr. Warnes, because they consider the *principle,* cannot be too thoroughly impressed upon the public mind; in short, to use the words of the worthy Bishop of the Diocese (we quote from memory) "Experiments cannot be useless or unprofitable; if they do not answer the intended purpose in themselves, they are sure to lead, at one period or other, to something that will facilitate the progress of information."

This is already the case with respect to the compound, as we shall have occasion to explain in reference to the experiment made by Mr. Postle.

Your Committee will, however, return to the more immediate business of the meeting in question. The bullocks shewn at the previous meeting on the 19th of May last, with an eleven months' old calf, were again exhibited, and one of the former, together with the calf, were afterwrds slaughtered in order to prove the fattening properties of native produce when formed into compound. All agreed that the animals "died well," and that finer meat was never brought to market. They were shewn at this meeting, not as extraordinary fat beasts, but as specimens of what might be effected in a given time. They were in a very low condition when put into the boxes on the 15th of January, and on the 16th of July following were examined by competent judges, who considered them fit for the butcher, one in particular. It is evident from these experiments that cattle may be fattened in six months, and that two returns may be made in a year with judicious management. In order to ascertain whether calves could be fattened with profit on compound, and sent to London like running calves, Mr. Warnes had one of six months old placed in a box and treated as the bullocks. It was fatter than could have been expected for the time, and was killed on the day of the meeting.

The following are the particulars of the bullocks slaughtered :—— Devon bullock, purchased on the 8th of January last, at 9*l.* 15s. killed on the 28th of October instant, weighed 58st. 10lbs. (loose fat 8st. 7lbs.) value of the carcase, at 8s. per stone, 23*l.* 10s. from which, after deducting the cost price, and 8*l.* 11s. for compound, leaves a balance of 5*l.* 4s. together with the manure, which may be set off against turnips and grass, the real value of which was trifling, on account of the small quantity consumed. The eleven-month-old calf was purchased in May, at 3*l.* of a dealer. It weighed 29st. 12lbs. loose fat, 4st. 2lb.) value of the carcase, at 8s. per stone, 12*l.* leaving a balance of 9*l.* for compound and grass; latterly it had a few potatoes and turnips, but no milk or any other food whatever.

In the booth were exhibited, numerous samples of linseed, flax in the straw, and specimens of wrought flax, all of Norfolk growth, together with sundry other productions, amongst which were the following :—

Twelve white carrots, taken in separate parts off the field, weight from three rods, 60st. 4lbs.; another sample of twelve white carrots, grown without muck, on wheat stubble, weight from three rods, 37st. 11lbs. when topped; another sample of twelve red carrots, grown also without manure, on wheat stubble, weight from three rods when topped, 19st. 7½lbs.; three Belgian carrots, weight 12¼lbs. beside many other extraordinary fine specimens of beet root, mangel wurzel, turnips in every variety, linseed, and different descriptions of grain and pulse, amongst the latter a specimen of lentile, or Egyptian vetch.

About three o'clock the company collected from various parts of the ground, and assembled in the booth to consider the desirableness of forming a Society, to extend and improve the cultivation of flax.

E. Wodehouse, Esq. M.P. was called to the Chair, and in opening the proceedings, said, if a knowledge of the subject respecting which the meeting had been convened was required in the chairman, he was not the person who should preside, but in common with every one present he felt that the cultivation of flax was a matter of deep interest, and therefore he would not detain the meeting with any lengthened observations of his own. He had taken the chair in obedience to Mr. Warnes' wishes, and would call on him to state his views.

Mr. Warnes rose and said, I rejoice that the time is arrived to which I have looked forward with so much anxiety. I rejoice at finding myself surrounded by so large an assembly, in number far exceeding my most sanguine expectations. But above all do I rejoice at beholding gentlemen whose advantages of education, station, and circumstances of life qualify them so well to take a comprehensive view of those plans which I shall have the honour of laying before them, and also to afford that vigorous assistance which alone can ensure success. I stand not here to advocate any selfish claims, but to lay before you ideas which have occupied my mind for some months past, arising from the difficulties into which the agriculture of this country is plunged by the alteration of the corn law and the tariff, involving alike the interests of the landowner, the occupier, and the labourer. Sir, we are arrived at a crisis fraught with alarming consequences to the community at large, such as render it the duty of every man who has, or thinks he has, a remedy to propose, boldly to come forward and declare it. Upon this principle I venture to claim your attention for a short time. There are some things connected with the late enactments over which we can exercise no controul ; but there are others over which we most certainly can. For instance, we cannot prevent the miller from purchasing foreign wheat, the baker from purchasing foreign flour, the merchant barley, or the manufacturer and the mechanic meat. But we can controul the indirect purchase of those very articles in the shape of foreign manure and of foreign cake. No one has a right to complain who will not refuse to purchase indirectly those articles the direct introduction of which he much condemns. But we are not now assembled to discuss the merits of cattle compound *versus* foreign oil cake ; our object is to take into consideration the desirableness of forming a society to extend and improve the growth of flax. For this purpose have those specimens been collected from various growers, principally between North Walsham and Norwich. They are placed before you in order that the discussion may in some measure be assisted by the practical illustration which they afford. There is nothing very striking in the appearance of these sheaves beyond their novelty; nor with respect to the beauty of the seed. But when we enquire into their properties and the various uses to which they can be applied to the service of man, we are struck with wonder and admiration. A society was formed in Ireland last year similar to that which I wish to see established in this county. I had seen some extracts from its proceedings, but wanted more authentic information, which Mr. Bacon, Jun. kindly undertook to obtain. Accordingly a letter was dispatched to

Mr. Skinner, the Secretary. That gentleman however had seen an account of our having grown so many acres of flax, and anticipating our lack of knowledge in preparing it properly for market, sent a parcel of pamphlets and papers containing the required particulars to the Norwich Mercury Office, with a letter to the Editor strongly advising the formation of a Flax Society here, and urging him to promote so desirable an object through the influence of his (the Mercury) paper. Now Mr. Bacon and Mr. Skinner were perfectly unacquainted with each other, and therefore it must at least be looked upon as a very singular coincidence that one gentleman should have been writing in England for certain papers and documents, which the other was at the same time engaged in forwarding from Ireland. Thus the parcel crossed the letter of application on the passage between the two kingdoms, and safely arrived in Norwich. This interesting occurrence affords a striking illustration of that warm-heartedness for which the Irish have ever been famed, and is a further proof of the advantages to be derived from our corresponding with that friendly nation. It appears that the same assistance and information which the Flax Society of Ireland obtained at considerable expence from Belgium, may be obtained by us at much less inconvenience and cost. The Secretary states that " the term of the engagement of the Belgian labourers having expired, three of these men are about setting out for their own country ; but we learn that some of them are so well pleased with Ireland that they are willing to re-engage with any party, for a month or two, who may require their services, on more moderate terms than those which induced them to come over. As their travelling expences to Belgium are paid by the Society, this is an opportunity that those should avail themselves of who have large scutch mills at work, or any handling of flax to get through."

Notwithstanding the immense advantages derived from the seed, cake, oil, and chaff, evidently the greatest centre in the fibre. There are only two specimens of flax on the table, which I had not seen when growing on the land. They were mostly grown on soils varying materially in quality. The sheaf which I now take up was grown by the Hon. Mr. Rous, on land of first-rate quality. The next which I shall offer to your notice, is a sample from five acres grown on the estate of the Right Hon. Lord Wodehouse, at Witton. When I tell you that the land is barely worth eighteen-pence an acre to rent, you can form a pretty correct idea of the quality, and yet observe here is an abundance of seed, and although the stalk is short, yet so exquisitely fine is the fibre, that the eye can no more discern the finest parts when drawn forth, than it could the floating cobweb. Its worth I cannot tell, but it appears to me well adapted for making bank notes; and perhaps his Lordship will feel gratified at the idea of this hitherto worthless land of his being appropriated to so good a purpose; at all events I hope that our Noble Friend and Member of the North Walsham Farmers' Club will order another trial to be made on similar land next year. I must now call your attention to the wrought flax, a specimen from my last year's crop. It was brought to that state in which you see it, in Yorkshire. Mr. Burton, from that county, paid me a passing visit last summer, to examine my crops of linseed, with others in the neighbourhood. He expressed himself surprised and gratified at what he had seen, and strongly advised us to persevere in our attempts; and as a proof of his sincerity, he took back, in the same steam packet with himself, a bundle of my flax in the stalk, had it prepared, and sent to this meeting for general inspection. As this crop is prized by foreigners and termed their golden crop, I can see no earthly objection to our striving for a little of that precious commodity ourselves, instead of allowing the Belgians to line their purses at our expense. But there is one subject to which I wish more particularly to allude, namely, the employment which the cultivation of flax would afford to the poor, than which a greater or more important object cannot engage the minds of men; and with respect to the growth of flax, I am sure that for every shilling I put into the poor man's pocket ten will be returned to my own. Useful and honest occupation for the labouring hand may almost be considered at this time the nation's desideratum; and yet I learn that there are annually sent out of this kingdom from ten to twenty millions of money to purchase flax, cake, oil, &c. all of which could be produced from the resources of our soil, and from the employment of our own rather than foreign labourers. The Irish have established a society to promote and encourage the growth of flax, and it is difficult to imagine upon what pretence objections can be made to the formation of a similar society in this county, which would have for its object the advancement of our own interests through the employment of the poor. To accomplish so desirable an aim, our legislators have for years held consultations and established laws, all of which have utterly failed. What they have laboured for in vain, you have now an opportunity of effecting. Regret not the singular facility of pleasing all parties, for should our endeavour be crowned with success, the Queen will be the first to rejoice at hearing that a means have been successfully resorted to for the relief of her suffering subjects—our senators will rejoice to find themselves delivered from the endless fatigue of framing poor laws—the philanthropist will rejoice to see his countrymen emancipated from the union workhouses, alike vexatious to them and burdensome to us—the christian philosopher will rejoice to see the labouring man once again occupied in earning his bread by the sweat of his brow; and lastly, how great will be the rejoicing of those innumerable poor who languish in idleness and misery, for the want of that aid which it is in your power to grant !

H. C. Partridge, Esq. had the honor of moving a resolution. They had all heard Mr. Warnes' clear and satisfactory statements, which had relieved him (Mr. Partridge) from going into details. He could have given but little information on the subject under consideration, and Mr. Warnes had given ample details respecting the growth of flax in that neighbourhood. The matter had been a great deal talked of and discussed, and they were all acquainted with Mr. Warnes' suggestions and statements. Everybody would allow that it should be an object of the farmer to increase his produce at the least expense. He (Mr. Partridge) knew no better way than by obtaining an ample and cheap supply of manure. Mr. Warnes said that cattle can be fed at home without the expense of foreign oil cake. If a proper and sufficient supply of fattening materials could be obtained at home, it was most desirable. From the new compound a greater proportion of manure could be obtained than at present. If every farmer grew linseed to mix with barley, his supply of manure would be greater than if he had to apply to a neighbouring merchant. As to the growth of linseed, they had seen the specimens that had been grown in that neighbourhood, and therefore there was no lack of information. He (Mr. Partridge) had his attention drawn to it by a paragraph in the newspaper; he immediately ordered a small portion to be sown in very bad land. One or two of the specimens of the produce had been exhibited, and as far as his judgment went, it was a crop that would pay better than any crop of corn that could be grown. In conclusion he should move—" That as the soil and climate of England are highly suitable for the growth of flax, it is resolved that a Society shall be formed to promote the cultivation of that important plant in Norfolk, having for its object the advancement of agriculture, and the finding employment for the poor."

Mr. Norfor seconded the resolution. He could not tell how the proposed cultivation of flax might answer in this county, but as regarded soil and climate, there was no reason why the plant should not be grown. The system of cropping proposed by Mr. Warnes would vary the cultivation of the land, and we all know that a frequent repetition of any grain on the same soil has a tendency to diminish the produce; it is therefore most unreasonable to suppose that the introduction of linseed, as an intermediate crop, would, even in this particular, be of some importance. Mr. Warnes had alluded to the employment of the poor. He (Mr. Norfor) had taken notice of the production of linseed, and the several methods adopted for disposing of the same, in various parts of the Continent, and in his opinion, however desirable it might be to imitate the Belgians in the cultivation of flax upon an extensive scale, as a marketable commodity, it is still more important to imitate the Swiss in making it subservient to the domestic economy of the labouring population in the country. In many parts of Switzerland every cottage has its small plot of flax, the preparation of which, after it is pulled, chiefly devolves upon the women and children. The whole process of preparing the fibre, down to that of weaving it into coarse cloth for domestic purposes, is performed by them at their own homes; and the several processes fill up the measure of industry through every period of the year, at intervals not otherwise appropriated to the more important duties of the household.

Sir Fowell Buxton proposed the next resolution. The Chairman had said he was not possessed of information on the subject under discussion. (He Sir F. Buxton) would not yield to any man in ignorance respecting it. (A laugh.) He came to listen and to learn, and he was deeply interested in the statements which had been made. There was one part of the statement that he was not quite so gratified with, viz. that the proposed cultivation of flax would cause a certain increase in the price of barley, particularly when Mr. Warnes indulged a hope of barley being raised to a guinea per coomb. Now to a man who consumed about a hundred thousand quarters of barley in the year, this was no very pleasing prospect. There were other points on which he heartily concurred; and none so much as that of providing employment for the poor. He was ignorant on other points, but he knew that labourers required employment. He hoped there would be no difference of opinion on this subject. They were all under considerable obligations to Mr. Warnes, and the least they could do was to raise the means by which the purposes of the Society could be carried out. He moved—

"That as funds will be required to further the ends of the Society, it is resolved that a list be now opened for donations and subscriptions; and that the public be invited to unite in furthering the laudable objects of the Society."

Mr. Clowes seconded the resolution. It would be superflous for for him to say anything further in favour of the resolution. He agreed with Mr. Warnes that the present was an important crisis. There was one question that particularly concerned those present as tenants, viz. the question of leases. This was a question that must not be neglected. Many leases would not allow tenants to grow flax on their farms. Some landlords might overloook this part of their leases. It would be for their interest in every way to grow linseed. He was sure they would all agree with him that liberal landlords made good tenants, and that by liberal covenants alone could the farmer meet the foreigner at the present prices. With these observations, he would second the resolution, which was carried unanimously.

W. Burroughes, Esq. proposed the next resolution. The subject had been so ably discussed, that he had only to move—

"That the Society shall be conducted by a President, Vice-President, Committee, Treasurer, and Secretary."

Mr. H. Playford had great pleasure in seconding the motion, which was carried *nem. con.*

The Chairman—In compliance with a suggestion from Mr. Warnes, he would recommend that the meeting be adjourned to the Bear Inn. But he must avail himself of that opportunity of expressing, in common with every person present, the great pleasure he had experienced in hearing the statements made by Mr. Warnes; and he was gratified also with the corroboration these statements had received from others. The Hon. Gentleman was convinced that there never was a subject more deeply interesting nor more important to the welfare of this county than the one which had been discussed. The present was a critical time for all engaged in agriculture. It seemed to him the proposed cultivation of flax held out a fair prospect of remuneration; and there was that above all other considerations, the prospect of removing the difficulty of providing permanent employment for all descriptions of labourers. He begged pardon for having made these remarks, and moved that the further consideration of the subject be adjourned till after the dinner.

The meeting then separated, and a number of the gentlemen proceeded to examine the animals that had been slaughtered in an outhouse, and the fattening properties of the compound appeared to be considered clearly proved; inasmuch, that H. N. Burroughes, Esq. M.P. in apologising for not being able to attend the meeting at an earlier period of the day, stated that he was in time to see and admire the bullock when killed; also the eleven months' old calf, fattened on the food that is likely to supersede foreign produce. His best wishes attended the measure, as also the success of the North Walsham Farmers' Club, the promoters of the pudding manufacture.

It will appear from the foregoing statements that the object of your Committee has been not only to furnish a report of the proceedings relative to the introduction of compound as an article of cattle food, but also to afford a detailed account of the circumstances which led to the cultivation of linseed, inasmuch as it originated with the North Walsham Farmers' Club, and they have now recounted the proceedings down to that period which ended in the formation of " The Norfolk Flax Society." Nor should they omit to notice that the columns of the Norfolk Chronicle as well as those of the Norwich Mercury, have been put in requisition to facilitate their labour.

Your Committee will now proceed to investigate the very important experiment instituted by Mr. J. Postle, of Smallburgh, with a view to determine the merits of compound *versus* oil cake.

COMPOUND *versus* OIL CAKE.

Statement of Consumption and Expense of Mr. Postle's *Short-horn Beasts, fed on Native Compound and Foreign Oil Cake.*

The Twelve Beasts were placed in the Yard, and fed on White Turnips, from Dec. 15th to the 20th; from Dec. 20th to the 2nd of January, on Swede Turnips, but these Turnips were not weighed.

Week ending the	9th of January—Weight of Turnips	,,	1351 stones	3 lbs.
,,	16th ,, ,,	,,	1279 ,,	5
,,	23rd ,, Six Compound Beasts		638 ,,	3
,,	—— ,, Six Oil Cake do.	,,	603 ,,	10

COMPOUND BEASTS.

		stones.	lbs.		lbs.		lbs. Per Week.
Jan. 30	Turnips per week	560	8	Compound	7	each per day, give	294
Feb. 6	,,	500	3½	,,	10	,,	420
13	,,	460	0	,,	—	,,	420
20	,,	439	12¼	,,	—	,,	420
27	(Cold and wet)	474	5¼	,,	—	,,	420
Mar. 6	,,	422	8¾	,,	14	,,	588
13	,,	422	8¾	,,	—	,,	588
20	,,	439	12¼	,,	—	,,	588
27	,,	405	5¼	,,	—	,,	588
Apr. 3	,,	396	10½	,,	21	,,	882
10	,,	405	5¼	,,	—	,,	882
17	,,	388	1¾	,,	—	,,	882
24	,,	388	1¾	,,	—	,,	882
May 1	,,	405	5¼	,,	—	,,	882
8	,,	378	6¾	,,	—	,,	882
15	Hay 42 stone	285	13½	,,	—	,,	882
22	42 do.	294	5¼	,,	22¼	,,	945
29	42 do.	292	7	,,	—	,,	945
June 5	50 do.	267	6	,,	—	,,	945
12	Hay and Grass.			,,	—	,,	945
15	do.			,,	—	,,	405
	Stones	7628	1			lbs.	14,485

OIL CAKE BEASTS.

		stones	lbs.		lbs.		lbs. Per Week.
Turnips	,,	569	0	Oil Cake	2	each per day, give	84
	,,	508	12¼	,,	3	,,	126
	,,	474	5¼	,,	—	,,	126
	,,	439	12¾	,,	—	,,	126
	,,	483	0	,,	—	,,	126
	,,	439	12¼	,,	5½	,,	231
	,,	422	8¾	,,	—	,,	231
	,,	439	12¼	,,	—	,,	231
	,,	422	8¾	,,	—	,,	231
	,,	422	8¾	,,	8½	,,	357
	,,	414	0	,,	9	,,	378
	,,	396	10½	,,	—	,,	378
	,,	388	1¾	,,	—	,,	378
	,,	405	5¼	,,	—	,,	378
	,,	378	6¾	,,	—	,,	378
Hay 42 stone		285	13½	,,	—	,,	378
42 do.	,,	294	5¼	,,	11	,,	462
42 do.	,,	292	7	,,	—	,,	462
50 do.	,,	267	6	,,	—	,,	462
	Hay and Grass.			,,	—	,,	462
	do.			,,	—	,,	198
	Stones	7745	10½			lbs.	6183

SUMMARY.

14 cmbs. 2½ bush. of Peas, at 14s. 6d. per cmb			£10 12 0¼
4 2¼ Linseed, at 25 6 "			5 17 11¼
Peas grinding	1 0 0 "		0 14 7½
Linseed do.	2 0 0 "		0 9 3
Making Compound . . .			1 0 0
3½ hundred Thorns, at 5s. per hundred . .			0 17 6
			£19 11 4¼
Deduct for 3½ bush. of Wood Ashes } at 1s. 6d. per bush. . .			0 5 3
			£19 6 1½
Balance in favour of Compound .			£2 8 7½

SUMMARY.

January 2, 1843—One ton of Dieppe Linseed Cake . .	£8 3 0
March 17, Ditto . .	7 15 6
April 28, 15 cwt. 1 stone, 9 lbs. at £7. 13s. per ton	5 16 3
	£21 14 9

The following Beasts are placed on the respective lines as they were divided by Mr. Wells, of Sco Ruston, and Mr. Heath, of Ludham; great attention being paid at the time to aptitude for Fattening, and it was determined by lot which should be fed on Compound.

COMPOUND BEASTS.

	Live Weight when Selected January 13th, 1843.	Live Weight when Fat June 17th.	Dead Weight, as received from Mr. Chapman, St. Giles', Norwich.		
	st.	st.	st. lbs.	st. lbs.	st. lbs.
No. 1, Weight	108	128	76 7	Loose Fat 11 1	Hide 7 1
2 "	98	117	71 2	" 8 5	" 6 9
3 "	100	119	70 4	" 9 4	" 6 3
4 "	100	120	71 8	" 9 7	" 6 9
5 "	100	125	72 8	" 8 8	" 6 5
6 "	96	116	70 6	" 8 12	" 6 7
	602	725	432 7	55 9	39 6
			55 9 loose fat		
			39 6 hides		

Stones 527 8 compound fed
Do.   477 2 oil cake fed

Stones 50 6 differ. in favour of Compound.

OIL CAKE BEASTS.

	Live Weight when Selected January 13th, 1843.	Live Weight when Fat June 17th.	Dead Weight, as received from Mr. Chapman, St. Giles', Norwich.		
	st.	st.	st. lbs.	st. lbs.	st. lbs.
No. 1, Weight	102	120	66 4	Loose Fat 8 2	Hide 6 3
2 "	94	113	62 6	" 8 0	" 5 12
3 "	98	121	67 0	" 9 7	" 6 6
4 "	96	116	60 4	" 9 5	" 6 6
5 "	100	118	66 3	" 8 10	" 6 10
6 "	100	117	65 9	" 7 10	" 6 4
	590	705	387 12	51 7	37 11
			51 7 loose fat		
			37 11 hides		

Stones 477 2

[N.B.—The respective weights are taken at 14 lbs. to the stone.]

D

Your Committee have heretofore described the process recommended by Mr. Warnes for the manufacture of " compound," and will now proceed to describe the method employed by Mr. Postle in fabricating " cake," which in contradiction to " French Cake," " Dutch Cake," and " London Cake," they will call " Club Cake," in honour of the Society from which it emanated. There are two cauldrons of thirty-six gallons each, one of which is adapted for heating with coals, and the other with wood or thorns. The former is the most expensive fuel, because thorns are the production of farm hedge rows, and are of but little value, but is nevertheless far preferable to the latter, because a more regular heat can be kept up with coals and with less attention on the part of the person engaged in the preparation of the ingredients.

The process is as follows :—

To fifteen gallons of water put one stone of linseed meal, and after this is boiled to a pulp of a jelly-like substance, add by little and little, four stones weight of pea or bean meal, or a mixture of both, together with inferior wheat, or any other grain at the option of the parties; this is to be well stirred in and incorporated by means of an iron grubber, such as is shewn in the annexed wood-cut, constructed somewhat like a spade, with open ribs. The process of incorporating the mass occupies about twenty minutes, when it is ready to transfer to the moulds. The fire being damped or wholly removed in order to prevent the mass from adhering to the bottom of the vessel, it is taken out with a large spatula, somewhat similar to a bricklayer's trowel, and transferred to the moulds prepared for the purpose; in doing which care must be taken to remove it from the sides of the cauldron first, rather than from the middle, otherwise as it cools it adheres like glue to the iron vessel. The moulds are constructed in sets of seven each, comprised in a frame about three feet six inches long, nine inches wide, and two inches and a half deep, the divisions of which are four inches and a half apart, consequently each cake is about the size of a brick.

This frame, of which the annexed wood-cut will convey an idea, is open at the top and bottom, and is placed on a flat board (for the purpose of being filled) in all respects similar to a brick-maker's table and mould, except that seven cakes are made at the same instant instead of one brick.

The dough (if we may so call it) is suffered to remain in the moulds a short time to cool and shrink, which it does sufficiently to admit of the frame being removed, thus leaving the cakes perfectly compact in the form of a well-made brick. They are then placed upon a splined rack, in a building through which there is a current of air from two latticed windows.

In three days it is sufficiently firm to admit of its being removed to any distance for use, and with a moderate degree of care it may be handled or packed together in a cart without injury even to its appearance.

The quantity of compound contained in one cauldron, as before described, is sufficient to fill eight moulds, and consequently makes about 54 or 56 cakes. These, when three days old, weigh about three pounds three or four ounces each. It will be observed that in the foregoing statement relative to the bullocks grazed by Mr. Postle, that their allowance was increased from 7 lbs. to $22\frac{1}{4}$ lbs. each per day; whereas during the same period the allowance of oil cake to their competitors was from 2 lbs. to 11 lbs. each. The same proportion is still adhered to, not only by Mr. Postle, but other persons who are now pursuing the system of supporting the British farmer, rather than that of foreigners and strangers.

The balance in favour of the compound (as shewn in the statement published by Mr. Postle) was not very material with regard to the cost price of either the one or the other, but there was an extraordinary difference in the value of the cattle fed with compound, over those which had been fattened on oil cake; consequently, although there may be a greater disproportion between the price of oil cake, and the expence of manufacturing the compound this year over that of the last in favour of oil cake, still the balance will be decidedly on the side of compound under general circumstances. There is one argument made use of by those who are opposed to this new method of grazing, which is so futile in itself that it cannot be too strongly reprobated, namely, the *trouble*. Now trouble is but another name for labour, and labour is the moving principle in the acquirement of wealth; it contributes to the well-being of the lower order of society; and it accelerates the accumulation of property in the higher grades; in short the benefit is mutual between the employer and the employed.

That the different substances made use of as articles of cattle food are more or less nutritious in proportion to the quantity of farinacious, saccharine, or oleaginous matter which they contain, is a subject every farmer is able to comprehend; but it has also been shewn in an admirable lecture delivered by Mr. John Coleby, Surgeon, at the North Walsham Farmers' Club Meeting, Nov. 17th, 1842, that cooked food has an immense advantage over that which is given in a crude state in the nourishment of animals. The following is the substance of Mr. Coleby's speech on this occasion :—

Mr. President and Gentlemen—In compliance with the request of several of my friends connected with this Club, I have the honour to appear before you this evening, for the purpose of offering to your notice some brief explanation of the process of digestion, more especially in reference to the nutritious properties of the compound which has of late so much engaged the public mind.

Food that has been retained in the stomach for a given length of time undergoes certain changes, it is reduced more or less to a fluid state, it is in other words digested ; it is subsequently endowed with the principle of life, and becomes a part of the body of the animal into whose stomach it has been received.

In order that you may comprehend these wondrous and important changes or operations, I propose to explain to you, in the first place, in a very succinct manner, the organs immediately engaged in digestion, and to point out certain remarkable peculiarities in the digestive organs of omnivorous animals, and those of herbaceous feeders. Secondly, to consider the nature and quality of food ; and thirdly, to describe to you the process of digestion, and the application thereof to the compound.

The mouth is the receptacle for food, and in carnivorous animals it is furnished with teeth for cutting and tearing the food, whilst in graminivorous animals, on the contrary, the teeth are particularly adapted for grinding the food. Connected with the mouth are glands, more especially developed in herbaceous feeders, for the secretion of the saliva, the saliva being poured into the mouth like little fountains, and thus mastication is completed ; the masticated food passes from the mouth by means of a tube termed " Oesophagus" to the stomach. I exhibit a diagram of the human stomach. You will observe the opening into the stomach where the food passes into the organ, and also the opening where the food is transmitted into the bowels.

Without entering into any minute anatomical description of the stomach, suffice it to say, that from its internal surface a fluid is secreted termed "gastric juice," which is of the highest importance to digestion.

There are two kinds of herbaceous feeders, those that ruminate as the ox, and those that do not, as the horse. I exhibit the upper and interior extremity of the stomach of the horse, for the purpose of shewing you a valve, which offering no impediment to the entrance of the food into the stomach, effectually prevents the return of any portion, and it is on this valve that the horse's total inability to vomit depends.

I now exhibit to you a diagram of the digestive apparatus of a ruminating animal, and instead of one stomach you will observe there are four. I will now explain to you how rumination is performed. Food that is devoured in large quantities by the animal undergoes but little mastication, and is conveyed through the oesophagus to the first stomach (shewn in No. 1 of the annexed diagram)—

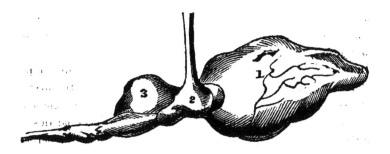

called pannel: the food undergoes little change in this stomach, except that of being slightly softened: from this stomach it passes in small quantities to the second stomach, (No. 2,) where it always meets with a portion of water; it is here rolled into a ball, thrown up through the oesophagus into the mouth, and undergoes a second mastication, it is then returned by the same tube into the third stomach, (No. 3,) where it undergoes the first chemical process of digestion, and from this stomach it is conveyed to the fourth and last stomach, (No 4,) where digestion is completed.

OF THE NATURE AND QUANTITY OF FOOD.

All food, whether animal or vegetable, notwithstanding the endless diversity of appearance, and whatsoever form it may be converted into, essentially consists of only three staminal principles. All food consists, or is composed of, a sweet or saccharine, an oily or oleaginous, and an albuminous principle. The two first are familiar to you, but not so, perhaps, the word albumen—all animal food contains albumen, and the white of an egg consists of pure albumen mixed with water.

All vegetables used for food contain two of these principles, viz.—the saccharine and oleaginous, whilst every part of an animal contains at least oil and albumen. The only substance prepared by nature expressly for food is milk. We therefore should expect to find in milk a perfect model of nutritious matter. Now it is a remarkable fact, that milk from every animal contains a saccharine, an oily, and an albuminous principle, and although these three principles are in different proportions in different animals, yet the three principles are always present.

Process of Digestion.

I shall now proceed to describe to you the process of digestion. The food having undergone mastication in the mouth, is conveyed to the stomach; in the stomach it meets with the gastric juice, which dissolves or reduces it to a more or less fluid state. The stomach has also the power to change the simple and nutritious principles into one another. Thus it would appear the stomach has the power to change or convert the saccharine principle into the oily, and the oily into the albuminous, or *vice versa*, the albuminous into the oily or saccharine, so that the production would be one uniform substance, to which life is afterwards imparted. So that the operations of the stomach may be divided into three grand processes.

Firstly, that of reduction—Of reducing the alimentary substances into more or less a fluid state. Secondly, that of conversion—Of converting the principles into one uniform substance. And thirdly, that of vitalization, or organization—To endow the nutritious principles with life. The two first appear to be chemical operations; the last arises from vital agency, and is not chemical.

The alimentary substance having passed into the upper part of the bowels, the innutritious is separated from the nutritious, and whilst the innutritious passes down into the bowels as excrementitious, the nutritious is taken up by a number of vessels called absorbents, which begin with open mouths from the internal surface of the bowel, and these eventually convey their contents to one vessel about the size of a quill, situated upon the lower part of the back bone. It then ascends along the spine to the neighbourhood of the heart, where it communicates with one of its large vessels. By this vessel it is carried to the heart, and afterwards circulated through the system for the future support, growth, and developement of the body.

The Compound.

I have already, when speaking of the nature and quantity of food, informed you that there are only three staminal principles of which all food can be composed, and as it may be here observed, that whilst *man*, an omnivorous animal, for the most part appropriates the three principles, the faculty of appropriation in graminivorous animals is under ordinary circumstances confined to two—viz. the saccharine and oleaginous. The compound now under consideration, being made up of barley and linseed previously ground and then subjected to a process of cookery, and so reduced to a pulp, contains the two principles before mentioned, and the superiority of an aliment so prepared, to food in a crude state, must be immediately apparent, when we reflect that the nutritious principles by culinary assistance become more fully developed—that is, that in a given weight a much larger proportion of nutritious matter is extracted and appropriated to digestion than could possibly be if taken in the crude state, and an assimilation for digestion effected with greater facility and less expense to the digestive organs. Food thus prepared may be profitably used in the case of all herbaceous animals, but there are, in my opinion, peculiar advantages to be derived from its use with regard to ruminating animals, which I shall endeavour to explain to you by reference to the diagram. Food that has been hastily swallowed, or is of an indigestible nature, is conveyed from the mouth to the first stomach, then to the second, where it is rolled into a ball, and in that form ejected into the mouth for the purpose of mastication, and when this process is completed, it is again conveyed by the same tube, not into the first, nor into the second, but into the third stomach. May it not then, I ask, be a fair subject for enquiry to ascertain whether food reduced by a culinary operation to a state similar to that in which it is left by mastication, would not be at once conveyed into the third stomach, in which digestion immediately commences. In corroboration of the truth of this theory, I am able to mention one well-established and indubitable fact—That milk swallowed by the sucking calf is conveyed immediately into the fourth and last stomach, and this is just what we should expect to find in an aliment attesting by its perfection the designing hand of Providence.

The only experiment I have as yet had an opportunity of making (though I intend most carefully to pursue my research), fully justifies me in the assertion that food having undergone the process I have already described, if not wholly, yet the larger portion of it is at once transmitted into the third stomach.

Mr. Coleby concluded his address in the following words :—We have this evening been engaged in the consideration of the relative value of cooked and crude food in the nourishment of animals ; we have seen in the course of our enquiry some striking and beautiful instances of the adaptation of the different organization of the animals to the circumstances under which they were designed to pass their lives, and we cannot but be attracted by the wise and beneficent provisions made by the hand of the great Creator to meet the every want of his creatures ; the farther we enquire the more will instances multiply, illustrating the same delightful fact ; but perfect as are all the arrangements of the universal economy, it does not follow that the use of artificial means may not facilitate certain processes upon which the nourishment of animals depend, and under certain circumstances the use of such means may be most important and valuable. The enquiring mind of man may be permitted to pursue its investigations in this field of research, without for an instant in the smallest degree appearing to indicate doubt of the wisdom and the beauty of the provisions which the great God of Nature has furnished to his every creature.

Sir Henry Durrant, Bart. being the chairman for the evening, moved a vote of thanks to Mr. Coleby, which was seconded by the Rev. Edward Wilkins, and met with great applause by the meeting.

It having been resolved that a good crop of turnips is of vital importance to the Norfolk system of farming, your Committee will now proceed to investigate the several discussions which have taken place under that head, and report to the Club the nature of the debates relative to the experiments which had been tried, in order to determine the best method of procuring the heaviest crops of that valuable root.

It was shewn by one of the members that he had made three experiments in the same field, in order to determine the proper distance at which turnips should be drilled on a flat surface. One part was drilled on ridges at 27 inches distance from each other, a second at 24 inches, and the remainder at 18 inches. Equal portions of the bulbs arising from each were weighed at the proper seasons, when it appeared that the result was in favour of the 24 inch drills over those of 27 inches, to the amount of 2 tons, 5 cwt. 5 st. and 10 lbs. per acre ; and in favour of 27 inches over 18 to the amount of 12 cwt. 6 st. and 12 lbs. per acre. The specific weight of each portion respectively being as follows :—

	WEIGHT OF BULBS.				WEIGHT OF TOPS.			
	Ton.	cwt.	st.	lbs.	Ton.	cwt	st.	lbs.
24 inch drills .	18	8	4	8	2	15	5	10
27 do. . . .	16	2	6	12	2	1	3	6
Difference	2	5	5	10	0	14	2	4
24 inch drills .	18	8	4	8	2	15	5	10
18 do. . . .	15	10	0	0	1	14	2	4
Difference	2	18	4	8	1	1	3	6
27 inch drills .	16	2	6	12	2	1	3	6
18 do. . . .	15	10	0	0	1	14	2	4
Difference	0	12	6	12	0	7	1	2

At a subsequent meeting some roots of a very large size and superior quality were exhibited, which had been grown in ridges 24 inches apart, the land having been manured with eight or nine loads of compost per acre, comprising the yard muck from bullocks fed on white turnips and oil cake, four chaldrons of quick lime and one ton of salt mixed together; but as it is not shown to what number of acres this compost was applied, the proportion which the latter substances bore to the whole amount of compost cannot be determined. Two varieties of turnips, the one purple and the other green were employed in this experiment with a view to ascertain if a greater weight of bulbs can be procured from one variety over that of another under circumstances where the quality of the land and the mode of preparing it for the reception of the seed are precisely similar; in this particular the green variety had so much the advantage in point of weight over the purple, that your Committee consider it very important to have experiments of the like nature prosecuted to an extent sufficient to determine the question, not only with regard to the distance at which turnips ought to be drilled, but also whether the same distance is applicable to every variety of that root; and moreover what varieties are the best adapted for the different soils in the vicinity to which the attention of the members is more particularly directed.

The result of the experiment in question appears to have been as follows :—

Purple—114 roots on a rod of land; weight per acre 14 tons 10 cwt. of bulbs, and 1 ton 10 cwt. of tops. Green—107 roots on a rod; weight 20 tons 11 cwt. 2 qrs. 20 lbs. of bulbs, and 1 ton 14 cwt. 2 qrs. 4 lbs. of tops, making a difference of 6 tons 6 cwt. 0 qrs. 24 lbs. in the weight of bulks per acre, in favour of the green variety over the purple.

Experiments had also been made to ascertain the extent to which artificial manures may be advantageously employed in the cultivation of turnips, from which the following result has been adduced, it being premised that the expence per acre was uniformly the same, viz. £2. 12s. 0d.

Weight of roots per acre, the land having been prepared with the following substances—

	Tons.	cwt.	sts.	lbs.
Ground Bones . . .	10	3	3	12
Yard Manure	12	7	2	3
Compost of fish scales and rich earth .	9	3	0	0
Guano	12	2	2	13
Rape Cake . ` . . .	8	18	5	4
Malt Culms	9	5	0	0
Sprats	9	11	7	0
Soil . . , . .	5	13	1	10

The small weight of bulbs compared with the statements laid before the public from others quarters excited much surprise amongst themselves, since they had been led to believe that it is no unusual circumstance for some land to produce as much as 40 tons per acre in the gross amount of tops and bulbs taken together, whereas out of all the foregoing experiments it would appear that 22 tons, 4 cwt. 5 st. 10 lbs. is the greatest weight that has been obtained in any one instance.

On the question of early and late sowing, some very large swedes were exhibited which had been sown on the 11th of May, and these compared with some others which had been sown later, shewed that the specific gravity of the one over that of the other was such as could not fail to denote the propriety of adopting a later period for putting in the general crop, although it may be desirable to have a few to be drawn off before the quality is determined. Upon the whole the impression appears to be, and in which your Committee coincide, is that the mean width at which turnips should be drilled is between 18 and 27 inches; that it greatly facilitates the growth of the plants to use some artificial manure in a powdered state to drill in with the seed, and that probably burnt ashes which had never been exposed to the atmosphere would be efficacious.

An investigation relative to the important subject of manuring for turnips was also brought before the notice of the Club; but as highly fermented or decomposed manure, and long muck fresh from the fold yard, had each its advocates, without any proof being adduced as to the efficacy of either the one or the other, the subject was deferred to some future period, when not only that but the comparative advantages of using artificial manure, such as crushed bones, rape cake, herring scales, lime and salt, might be brought under consideration; at the same time it appeared to be admitted that the practice of stall-feeding cattle under cover might be universally adopted, since it is unquestionable that the manure thus obtained is preferable to any other.

The best method of preserving turnips for spring use is a very important question, and one which engaged the attention of the Society. The several methods more particularly alluded to embraced the following :—viz. drawing them off the land on which they grow at any time after they have attained their full size, and placing them in a compact form upon some spot near the homestead simply with the root downward, and without ploughing or breaking the ground on which they are placed, or which was considered still better, to remove them to a piece of wheat or barley stubble, and there mould them up in furrows drawn by a plough, so that the whole land is occupied with the turnips which are thus placed nearly as compact as may be done by the former method, and by which means, i.e. by being covered with earth, they are better secured from frost, and retain their quality much longer. It is deemed advisable to have a portion of the crop ploughed in upon the land on which they grew, for the two-fold purpose of being more readily formed under a deep snow, and for the convenience of exposing the turned up soil to the action of frost during the winter months, and by this means saving one earth in the spring tillage.

The nature and properties of artificial grasses was a subject introduced by a member of the Club, upon which occasion a paper was read, the purport of which was as follows :—Grasses may be divided into two classes—those which are indigenous to the soil, and those that are extraneous or imported, which, by way of distinction, we will call artificial. It is of the greatest importance to make ourselves acquainted with the properties of the several varieties of grasses we are in the habit of cultivating, since it is unquestionable that some are adapted to one soil, and one mode of treatment, and some to another; and it must be a great proof of ignorance to sow all kinds of grass seeds on one description of land. For instance, sainfoin and lucerne, which are deep rooted grasses, require a considerable depth of soil to insure a plant, but more particularly the latter, of which I have noticed some striking peculiarities. If brick earth is too near the surface, and the soil naturally adhesive, the roots cannot penetrate sufficiently deep in the earth to procure that kind of nourishment which the plant requires, nor will it ever thrive, even if manure should be applied with unsparing liberality. On the contrary, if it is grown upon a deep loam, or what is commonly termed a good mixed soil, the plant thrives prodigiously, provided only a moderate degree of care is taken to eradicate weeds, and fork in a small quantity of manure occasionally between the ridges. Sainfoin is frequently grown on chalky land, and sometimes on that which is rather light, with a good depth of loose soil, but as it is not much cultivated here we will pass it by. Cow grass, which is a species of red clover, is also a deep rooted plant, and one which I can fully recommend to every farmer, but especially to those who farm on the six years' course of husbandry.

In the second year it frequently happens that the common broad-leaved red clover dies off, and sometimes the common rye-grass, which very seldom happens to cow grass—this will stand the second year, and be nearly as prolific as it was the first. It is a perennial grass, and will sometimes remain in the land for a very great length of time.

These deep rooted grasses derive a considerable portion of their nourishment from the subsoil, or that portion of the earth which has never been disturbed; their minute fibres penetrate to a very considerable depth, and as such they do not exhaust the soil nearer to the surface of the pabula which other plants require. This is one reason why they are so productive, and why they recommend themselves to our notice; they penetrate into a maiden soil; they absorb an indefineable something which other plants cannot reach, and they leave the land in a better state than any other grasses. I have grown heavier crops of hay from cow grass, even in the first year after sowing it, but in the second there is no sort of comparison between the bulk of hay which this grass will afford over red clover or any other grass whatever.

Perhaps it may be advanced as an objection to the cultivation of this plant, that the second crop or aftermath grass (as it is sometimes called) is not so heavy as that of clover. This I admit to be the case, but not to the extent which some people imagine. This circumstance may be easily accounted for; the stalk retains its juices longer than that of any other species of herbage, consequently at the period it is really fit to cut, it appears to be in the full vigour of its growth; this deter people from cutting it as soon as it should be, and the consequence is that the exhaustion to which the root is subjected prevents its putting forth new stems with sufficient vigour to arrive at maturity during that season. The practice of letting hay stand till the leaves are falling is a very bad one, and injurious to the crop, both with regard to quantity and quality. I cut my cow grass tolerably early, and by this means secure a sufficient second crop to mow in a green state for the working horses. If the cow grass grow less rapidly after cutting than clover, there is this advantage attending it, that it continues longer in a green state fit for soiling; in short it will wait for you (if I may be allowed to use such an expression), and thereby prevent a waste which might otherwise occur. Another advantage is, that, comparatively speaking, it is new to the land, consequently it produces a stronger and better plant, a plant that will stand where red clover would be almost sure to fail. Every one knows that a failure in the layer is almost sure to super-induce a failure in the succeeding crop of wheat. During the last two years in succession I have had my best wheats after cow grass, which fully convinces me that it is not an exhausting crop, an idea which can only be entertained from the bulk of hay which it pro-duces, but which is in no way proved by experience.

Red clover is imported from France and Germany, and as the climate of these countries is much warmer than that of our own, it is more congenial to its growth; nor does it succeed to any certainty upon our lands if sown at intervals of less than six years.

I have tried it an interval of five years, and have obtained a full plant; inasmuch that when the barley was cut, it had more the appearance of hay than corn; nevertheless, at the spring of the year following, the plants had died off to the extent that scarcely one was to be found in a yard of ground. As the clover either died off or was destroyed by the slug or other insects, it occurred to me that it could neither have exhausted the land or absorbed that kind of nutriment which clover requires; consequently I put on clover again, but it disappeared as before. Fortunately in both cases there was an intermixture of white clover, which in some measure supplied the deficiency. But in a case of a contrary description, relative to a piece of land which lately came into my occupation, which had not been laid down with red clover seed for very many years, the produce was so abundant that scarcely any rye grass or white clover were to be found, although the proportionate admixture of seed had been the same as in the former case. Highly cultivated land is no less likely to fail in producing a crop of clover than that on which less care had been bestowed, provided that sufficient pains had been taken to eradicate the weeds; therefore it does not appear that either the quantity of manure bestowed upon the soil, or the superior tillage to which it may have been subjected, has any material influence in securing the cultivator from the serious injury which he sustains from the loss of his hay crop.

Farmers in general have a very superficial knowledge of any thing relating to chemistry; still I am inclined to think that we know more of chemistry than we are aware of. What would our forefathers have thought of applying salt-petre as a top dressing to stimulate the growth of herbage? Why in all probability they would have imagined that pepper and mustard would be equally efficacious; nevertheless, however limited their knowledge may have been in the chemical properties of manure, there is one thing at least in which they surpassed the present generation; namely, that if they once laid hold of a guinea, they were wise enough to keep it. I have endeavoured to shew that all lands after a series of years (in the common acceptation of the term) become *tired* of clover, and I have only to suggest, that by way of experiment, a few perches of land in the midst of various fields should, previous to being laid down with clover seed, have a plentiful dressing of some maiden soil, even though it should be no better than sand, brick-earth, or gravel. Nor have I any doubt of a favourable result. An admixture of red and white clover is highly desirable, but that of red clover and trefoil is injudicious for many reasons, but more especially that in the next rotation the land would be ill adapted for both the one and the other, from the very reason before alluded to.

Notwithstanding a judicious admixture of grasses I conceive to be of very great importance, but more especially the several varieties of the rye grass intermixed with either clover or trefoil. The former approximate to the natural grasses, or those which grow spontaneously, and it is quite certain that cattle will always pick out the hedge-row grasses, or even the common spear grass before they have entirely consumed varieties on which they may happen to be depastured.

The subject of top dressing wheat and grasses was introduced and discussed, when a variety of opinions were expressed, all tending to prove that in this district top dressing wheat rarely repays the cost; there is decidedly more straw, but as the top dressing produces a disposition to mildew, the sample is injured, and the quantity of grain necessarily diminished.

The general opinion however seemed to be in favour of top dressings for grass lands; but although almost every member present had in some way or other top dressed either corn or grass, no one had proved the result with sufficient accuracy to arrive at any definite conclusion.

The following is the result of some experiments made with a view to ascertain the fertilizing properties of sundry manures used as top dressings upon layers of trefoil, white clover, and rye grass, the seed of which was mixed in the usual proportions.

These experiments were conducted by one of the members of the Club, upon land of a free working loamy quality, with a subsoil of brick-earth and field clay, and presented to the Society by the gentleman who conducted them, in a paper, of which the following is a transcript.

Having measured out six pieces of land, each one chain square and separated two yards from each other, to secure the experiment, they were on the 7th of April, 1841, sowed broadcast with the following manures, which subsequently produced the several quantities of hay, the weight of which is given in the following table :

No.	s.	d.	WEIGHT OF HAY. cwt.	qrs.	lbs.
1.—11½ lbs. of saltpetre, cost (carriage included)	3	3	5	2	0
2.—11¼ lbs. of nitrate of soda	2	8	5	0	0
3.—A one-horse cart-load of fish mould (about 1 ton)	2	0	4	3	23
4.—A one-horse cart load of horse yard manure	2	0	4	3	19
5.—Five bushels of salt and lime	5	0	3	3	8
6.—No manure	0	0	4	0	11

The hay was mowed, and strewed about on the morning of the 15th of June, and weighed on the 17th of the same month, in the afternoon. Having taken one-tenth of an acre for each experiment, and one-tenth part of each quantity of manure, if we multiply the before-mentioned results by 10, it will give the total amount per acre; which I will reduce to figures, and value my hay at 4s. per cwt. although I am now (April, 1842) selling it at 5s. 6d.

No.	s.	d.	PRODUCE. tons.	cwt.	qrs.	lbs.
1.—1 cwt. of saltpetre per acre, cost	32	6	2	14	3	18
2.—1 cwt. of nitrate of soda	26	6	2	9	3	18
3.—10 one-horse cart loads of fish mould	20	0	2	9	2	6
4.—10 one-horse cart loads of stable manure	20	0	2	9	0	22
5.—50 bushels of salt and lime	50	0	1	18	0	24
6.—No manure	0	0	2	0	3	26

I here find by comparing Nos. 1, 2, 3, and 4, with No. 6, after deducting all cost for manure and labour, that I gain by

No. 1	£1	3	5	per acre.
2	0	9	3	—
3	0	14	0	—
4	0	12	9	—

but as I get eleven shillings' worth less hay off of No. 5 than No. 6, and the cost of the manure being £2. 10s. I lose £3. 1s. by that acre.

I ought to explain the nature of the compost which I call " fish mould." In the summer of 1840 a large fish was thrown upon the sea beach, which weighed about three tons; it was a species of

Grampus, and required the aid of twelve horses to draw it to a field near at hand. It was there cut into pieces of about two stones each in weight, and disposed of in alternate layers of decomposed vegetable matter and earth mixed together, plentifully sprinkled with quick lime. Thus it remained for about six months, when it was turned over. At that time all appearance of the fleshy part of the fish was gone; about two months afterwards I used part of this compost in the experiment I have just detailed. The remainder has been turned over three or four times, some of which has been applied as a top dressing upon wheat and layer, and a small portion reserved for turnips by way of experiment. As to the salt and lime, in the early part of January, 1841, I procured 25 cwt. of common salt, at the cost of 1s. 8½d. per cwt. amounting in the whole to 36 bushels, and with this I mixed under the cover of a shed (one side of which only was open to the air) two chaldrons of fresh-burnt lime, making in all 108 bushels; during the first month I had this compost continually turned over, in order that it might be thoroughly incorporated, and during the last two months prior to its being used, it was turned only once or twice; in short, I followed the directions given in the 16th chapter, page 408, of "Johnson on Manures." I ought to have stated that the cost of the lime was 18s. a chaldron, and beside the prime cost, that of mixing, carting home and to the field, together with the sowing, must be placed to the account.

I will now turn to another field near to the former, and about the same distance from the sea. Here on the 13th of April, 1841, I sowed in plots also of one chain square, separated as before, the following manures; the produce from which is also stated.

No.	s.	d.	cwt.	qrs.	lbs.
1.—2½ bushels of salt and lime, cost	2	6	3	3	0
2.—23 lbs. of nitrate of soda	5	4	6	0	25
3.—23 lbs. of saltpetre	6	6	5	·2	15
4.—A one-horse cart load of fish mould	2	0	4	3	0
5.—A one-horse cart load of stable yard manure	2	0	3	1	9
6.—No manure	0	0	3	3	2

This hay was mowed and strewed on the morning of the 14th of June, and weighed on the 16th in the afternoon. Having previously described the several manures, I will only observe that in this field the land was quite as good as in the other, and that I here used half as much salt and lime only; and double the quantity of nitrate of soda and saltpetre, as also of fish mould and yard manure, as in the other. In the first field the experiments were made about forty yards from a fence having a south aspect, and running parallel with the several squares ; in the last mentioned field they were made on falling ground with a north aspect, and not near the hedge. The total productions were as follows :—

No.	s.	d.	tons.	cwt.	qrs.	lbs.
			Produce.			
1.—25 bushels per acre of salt and lime, cost	25	0	1	17	2	0
2.—2 cwt. of nitrate of soda	53	0	3	2	0	26
3.—2 cwt. of saltpetre	65	0	2	16	1	10
4.—10 one-horse cart loads of fish mould	20	0	2	7	0	2
5.—10 one-horse cart loads of yard manure	20	0	1	13	1	6
6.—No manure	0	0	1	17	2	20

On comparing Nos. 2, 3, and 4, with No. 6, I find myself a gainer, but by Nos. 1 and 5 I am a loser.

No. 2 gains	.	.	£1 13 0 per acre, net profit.
3	.	.	0 10 0 ditto
4	.	.	0 13 0 ditto

By No. 1, I get nine-penny worth less hay than by No. 6, which added to the cost of manure, gives a total loss of £1. 5s. 9d. ; and No. 5 compared with No. 6 shews a loss of 17s. 6d. in hay, which added to the cost of manure, produces a total loss of £1. 17s. 6d. The loss by No. 5, I attribute in a great measure to the manure not being put on in time to be washed in, and therefore the hay could not be cut so close to the ground as it ought to have been by two or three inches ; at the same time I think that the manures on Nos. 1, 2, and 3, would be quite as well sown in the early part of May, provided the weather is not too dry.

Previously to the hay harvest a great quantity of rain had fallen, and it occurred to me that this circumstance might have contributed to produce the difference shewn in the above statements. To prove this I put 1lb. of nitrate of soda in an earthen vessel, and added thereto 1lb. of rain water, the temperature of the water being at 46 degrees of Fahrenheit's thermometer, & that of the nitrate at 38 degrees, but upon covering the bell of the thermometer with the nitrate which had settled to the bottom, the mercury immediately fell to 30 degrees. I then tried it with saltpetre, putting 1lb. of this to an equal weight of water ; the mercury fell from 46 degrees to 43 degrees, and kept falling, on my adding more water, till there was five times its weight, at which time it stood at 38 degrees, and did not fall any lower even when the bell of the thermometer was covered with the saltpetre which had settled to the bottom of the vessel. From this circumstance I am led to conclude that saltpetre will be found of more service on strong wet lands than soda. The field in which the saltpetre answered the best, laid low and flat, and the water would naturally stand and settle through ; whereas in the other field, as the experi-

F

ment was tried on the slope of a hill, the water would run off, and here the nitrate of soda was found to answer the best of the two.

Thus I am led to believe that saltpetre will be found to be more efficacious on wet land than nitrate of soda: but that both the one and the other are more serviceable to dry land, and such as is liable to parch or scald in summer than where there is an excess of moisture.

Up to the present time I have not been able to discover any superiority in the appearance of the plant of wheat which is growing on the several departments where the manures have been tried; but it should be observed, this is only the experience of *one* year, and is not a fair criterion to judge by, since different soils and seasons may produce different results, and it is only by pursuing the subject in an experimental way for a series of years, that we can expect to arrive at anything like a satisfactory conclusion.

On the comparative advantages of employing oxen in farm labour instead of horses, it was shewn that an occupation which requires more than nine horses, or even more than seven horses, a saving of ten pounds a year is effected by using oxen. A horse fit for the purposes of husbandry can neither be reared nor purchased, at four years old, for less than twenty-five pounds; and supposing that he should remain at work for a period of ten years, he would decrease in value two pounds ten shillings annually—whereas a bullock, the cost price of which would not be more than one half of that sum, might be expected to increase in value annually to the same amount.

Another very important consideration relative to the use of oxen is, that they are less liable to disease, and moreover that an accident to the limbs which would render a horse perfectly useless might be of no material importance to an ox, since it may still be stall-fed and prepared for the butcher. With regard to the expense of feeding the one and the other, while at work, it might be admitted that the bullock and the horse when fed on grass would consume the same quantity of food, although it is unquestionable that any one would prefer having a bullock to keep rather than a horse; but in the winter season there is a very important difference in the expenditure for food between the horse and the ox, since the latter can be kept very well upon the hay only which would be required for the horse, thus effecting a saving of a bushel of oats per week, which for thirty weeks at 3s. 6d. amounts to no less a sum than five guineas, without taking into account the necessity of shoeing the horse, which the ox does not require, and the little attention bestowed upon the latter compared with that of the former.

On the other side it was contended that oxen were ill adapted for draught upon the hard road, although they might be used to advantage in field labour, and moreover that the hay stack was more profitably consumed by horses than oxen; again that the manure left by the horse is infinitely more fertilizing than that of the ox, and that horses would continue at work more than ten years upon an average, and consequently do not decrease in value to the amount of fifty shillings annually. This subject produced a very animated discussion, which terminated in the following decision: namely, that when the size and situation of the farm is suitable to the employment of oxen, they are decidedly to be preferred, since the cost price is less than that of the horse, the risk less, and the expense of keeping less, and that they annually increase in value up to a given age, about in the same ratio with which the horse decreases in value.

An enquiry into the relative advantages of cultivating land under what is called the four and six-course shift of husbandry respectively, was introduced to the notice of the Club, when it was contended by the member who advocated the latter, that by saving a portion of the wheat stubbles with the same grain the second year, the whole produce of the farm in wheat is equal to the whole produce of the same quantity of land cultivated in the four-course shift, and would leave the land in a better state than if barley had been taken without muck. He further contended that turnips produced after a clear interval of five years are generally worth a pound an acre more than those taken on the four-course shift after an interval of three years only. That the same remark is applicable to the hay crop also, since clover can always be taken without risk of failure under the six-course shift, and is always worth a pound an acre more than any other variety of grass. Less expense is also incurred in the purchase of seeds, since one-sixth of the whole occupation is annually laid down to grass instead of one-fourth. In short, that the difference in favour of the six-course shift over the four amounts to ten shillings an acre per annum, or a saving of £120 on a farm of 240 acres ! !

The four-course shift was as strongly advocated by other parties, when the question being put by the Chairman—

It was resolved, that soil and situation had so much to do with the courses of husbandry pursued in different districts, that it was impossible to determine which particular system could be recommended for general practice.

The utility of the subsoil plough, and the advantages or dis-advantages which had been ascertained to proceed from stirring the soil to a greater depth than can be effected by the common plough, without bringing up the barren earth to the surface, produced some interesting discussion. The idea of disturbing the substratum of arable lands had never been entertained by several of the members; and the statements of those who had practised the system by way of experiment was listened to with evident satisfaction: although it must be admitted that further proofs than those which were adduced are required before it would be prudent to pursue the system upon an extensive scale, still there appeared to be sufficient ground for the Club to adopt the following resolutions :—

1st. That the subsoil plough may be applied with advantage to all such land as requires to be under-drained.

2nd. That it is highly beneficial for breaking up tenacious and adhesive soils, hard pans, or beds of gravel lying near the surface; and

3dly. That it renders those fields, or portions of fields, more fertile which are subject to *scald* from any cause whatever.

Mr. Coleby and Mr. Mann severally delivered lectures on chemistry as applicable to agriculture; on the manner in which plants receive their nourishment; and on the nature of soils; but as the manuscript copies of these lectures were not laid before the Committee, they have not the means of inserting them.

At the meeting held Nov. 9th, 1843, the Committee presented their Report of the proceedings during the past three years, in accordance with a resolution of last year. The Report was adopted by the meeting, subject to the condition that Mr. Warnes should be allowed to strike out any part of his own observations reported therein, but not to make any alterations or additions thereto.

A vote of thanks to the Committee for the trouble they had taken to draw up the Report was moved and carried unanimously, and that the same should be recorded on the minutes of the Society.

GEORGE GOWER, Secretary.

Bacon, Kinnebrook, and Co. Mercury Office, Norwich.

ERRATA.

Page 8, last line but one—for *meal* read *meat.*

  „ 21, line 6—*most* read *not.*

  „ 34, line 30—*determined* read *deteriorated.*

  „ 35, line 21—*formed* read *found.*

  „ 41, lines 31 and 37—*bell* read *ball.*

  „ 43, line 19—*saving* read *sowing.*

CPSIA information can be obtained
at www.ICGtesting.com
Printed in the USA
LVHW110033110122
708206LV00007B/802